EXTREME WEATHER

TROPICAL STORMS AND HURRICANES

Liza N. Burby

The Rosen Publishing Group's
PowerKids Press™
New York

Published in 1999 by The Rosen Publishing Group, Inc.
29 East 21st Street, New York, NY 10010

First Edition

Book Design: Resa Listort

Photo Credits: p. 4 © Kevin Vandivier/Viesti; p.6-7 © Morgan Williams/Viesti; p. 8, 10-11 © Jack Zehrt/FPG; p. 12 © Thomas Kanzler/Viest; p.14-15 © Marianne Barcellona/Viesti; p. 16, 20 © Frank Siteman/Viesti; p 19 © Simons, Chip/FPG.

Burby, Liza N.
      Tropical storms and hurricanes / by Liza N. Burby.
           p. cm. — (Extreme weather)
      Includes index.
      Summary: An introduction to tropical storms and hurricanes with information on how they begin, when and where they occur, the damage they can do, and some of the worst storms of this century.
      ISBN 0-8239-5290-8
      1. Storms—Juvenile literature. 2. Hurricanes—Juvenile literature. 3. Tropics—Climate—Juvenile literature.
      [1. Storms. 2. Hurricanes. 3. Tropics—Climate.] I. Title. II. Series: Burby, Liza N. Extreme Weather.
QC941.3.B87 1998
551.55—dc21   98-19931
                                                                             CIP
                                                                             AC

Manufactured in the United States of America

Contents

What Are Tropical Storms and Hurricanes?

Tropical (TRAH-pih-kul) storms happen when rain and strong winds of about 40 to 70 miles per hour are stirred up over warm oceans. If they become stronger, with winds over 75 miles per hour, they are called hurricanes. Each year, more than 100 tropical storms occur all over the world. About 60 of them are strong enough to become hurricanes. Luckily, very few of them reach places where people live. But people who have lived through a hurricane know it is one of the most powerful forces of nature. **Meteorologists** (MEE-TEE-er-OL-uh-jists) call them Earth's mightiest storms.

Tropical storms and hurricanes will often hit warm coastal areas, or warm areas that are near the ocean.

Where and When Do They Happen?

Tropical storm and hurricane **season** (SEE-zun) is usually from June to November. The storms start in warm ocean waters around the **equator** (ee-KWAY-ter). In the Indian Ocean and around Australia, the storms are called **cyclones** (SY-klohnz). In the South Pacific and West Pacific Oceans, they are called **typhoons** (ty-FOONZ). In the Caribbean Sea, North Atlantic Ocean, and the Gulf of Mexico, they are called hurricanes. These are all the same kind of storm. The only place they do not form is in the South Atlantic Ocean. Scientists do not know why.

Sometimes hurricanes over land can cause tornadoes, such as this one that occurred in South Dakota, in 1914.

7

How Do They Start?

When ocean water gets warm it starts to **evaporate** (ee-VA-per-ayt) and becomes water **vapor** (VAY-per), or clouds of warm, wet air. These warm clouds move upward. More hot air rushes in from all sides to replace the rising air. In the middle of the rising air, a **column** (KOL-um) of sinking air forms. Winds begin to swirl. Then a storm begins. The warmer the ocean is, the stronger a hurricane is likely to become.

The center of a hurricane is called the eye. There is no activity there, and it is always calm. Outside of this eye is the eye wall, where the storm's winds are strongest. These winds blow the storm over the ocean.

The eye (center) of a storm is calm, but strong winds and rain surround it on all sides.

How Do These Storms Act?

Hurricanes are scary. Their winds shriek and howl. Pictures of them show that a hurricane can look like a doughnut or a pinwheel. Each one is about ten miles high and 300 to 600 miles wide. They move around and forward like a spinning top.

The size of a storm can be seen in radar photos such as this one. This storm spreads out far over the land below it.

When a hurricane starts, it usually travels slowly, about ten to twenty miles per hour. As it moves farther north, it speeds up to 60 miles per hour. A hurricane can travel hundreds of miles each day. But as it moves over land, it loses power because there is no more hot, wet ocean air to keep it going.

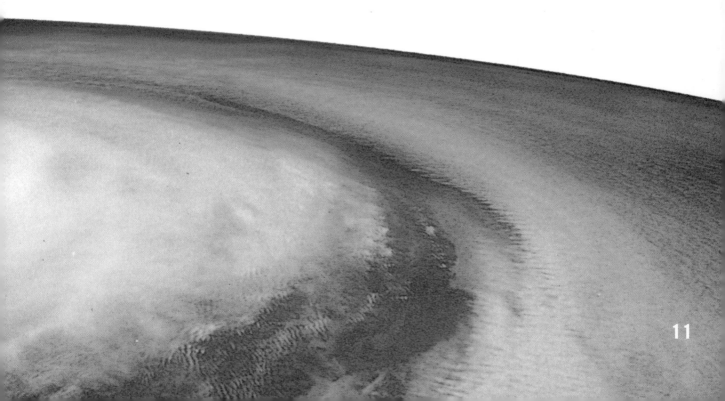

Why Are They Dangerous?

Tropical storms and hurricanes can be very dangerous. Strong storm winds are unsafe because they scoop up things like bicycles or even small trees. These things can fly through the air and cause damage. Heavy rains often cause **flooding** (FLUH-ding). Sometimes six to twelve inches of rain will fall in a day during a tropical storm or hurricane. But the worst part of these storms is the storm **surge** (SERJ). A storm surge happens when the ocean rises several feet higher than usual and waves form on top of that. This huge swell of water crashes over land and can wash away homes and people. In 1900 more than 6,000 people drowned when a storm surge swept across Galveston, Texas.

Even homes and other buildings built high on a cliff may not be safe from a storm surge.

Strange Things They Can Do

Hurricane winds are so strong they can carry off whole forests. They yank roofs off houses and carry boats from the shore, dumping them on roads that are far away. Birds from the West Indies have been blown all the way to Florida in the United States. Hurricane winds can even make the walls of houses move in and out as if they were breathing.

Hurricanes have made whole towns disappear. In 1938 the Rhode Island town of Misquamicut was completely wiped away by winds. Afterward, it looked as if the town had never been there.

Hurricanes and their winds can cause severe permanent damage

Naming Tropical Storms and Hurricanes

Since 1953, meteorologists have given names to tropical storms and hurricanes so they can keep track of the storms. The first tropical storm of the season is given a woman's name starting with the letter "A." The second storm is given a "B" name, and so on through the alphabet. In 1979 men's names were added. Names are repeated every six years. If a storm is very wild, however, like Hurricanes Andrew and Camille, its name is never used again. In 1969 Hurricane Camille killed 256 people in the Mississippi Delta. In 1992, Hurricane Andrew killed 26 people in Florida and caused $25 billion in damage.

Hurricane Andrew's damage spread all along the East Coast, including this trailer park in Florida.

Predicting These Storms

Meteorologists are able to follow tropical storms and hurricanes by using **radar** (RAY-dar) and **satellites** (SA-tih-lyts). Weather balloons with measuring **instruments** (IN-struh-ments) that warn meteorologists of developing storms are sent around the world to spot changes in **temperature** (TEMP-ruh-cher) and water vapor.

Hurricanes can get stronger, faster, and change direction very quickly. For this reason, meteorologists will tell people about a hurricane watch about 36 hours before they **predict** (pre-DIKT) that a hurricane may hit land. A hurricane warning means the storm is likely to hit within 24 hours. A warning is more serious than a watch.

Doppler radar, like this one at the Randome National Severe Storm Center in Norman, Oklahoma, helps meteorologists predict when the next severe storm will occur.

Safety During a Tropical Storm or Hurricane

People who don't live near the ocean don't worry too much about the danger of tropical storms or hurricanes. But people who live where these storms hit should know what to do to stay safe. They should know about all the roads that lead **inland** (IN-lind) in case they have to leave in a hurry. They should have a battery-operated radio so they can follow weather reports. Plenty of clean, bottled water should be available. When people are told to **evacuate** (ee-VA-kyoo-ayt) an area, they should go right away.

Some hurricanes are so dangerous that surviving or staying safe during one is often something to be proud of.

Tropical Storms and Hurricanes Can Be Helpful

As scary as tropical storms and hurricanes can be, we actually need them. They help keep Earth's temperature from getting too hot. They bring rain to areas that are too dry. These falling rains also clean our air.

Many scientists believe Earth's temperature is going up. This is called global warming. If this is true, there may be more hurricanes in our future. But when towns, counties, and states plan ahead by planning evacuations and building walls to hold back the sea, more people will stay safe during Earth's mightiest storms.

Glossary

column (KOL-um) An object that is tall and thin.

cyclone (SY-klohn) A different name for a hurricane in some areas of the world.

equator (ee-KWAY-ter) An imaginary line around Earth that separates it into two parts, North and South. This area is always hot.

evacuate (ee-VA-kyoo-ayt) To leave quickly.

evaporate (ee-VA-per-ayt) When a liquid changes to a gas.

flooding (FLUH-ding) When there is too much water in an area and it runs over land that is usually dry.

inland (IN-lind) Land that is not near the water.

instrument (IN-struh-ment) Tool.

meteorologist (MEE-TEE-er-OL-uh-jist) A person who studies the weather.

predict (pre-DIKT) To know something before it happens.

radar (RAY-dar) A machine that is used to predict weather.

satellite (SA-tih-lyt) A machine in space that is used to predict weather.

season (SEE-zun) A special time of year when something happens.

surge (SERJ) A sudden strong rush of water.

temperature (TEMP-ruh-cher) How hot or cold something is.

tropical (TRAH-pih-kul) Having to do with a part of the world where it is hot and moist year-round.

typhoon (ty-FOON) A different name for hurricanes in some areas of the world.

vapor (VAY-per) Tiny water droplets in the air.

Index